Wildflowers

Brooklynn Hinkle

BookLeaf Publishing
India | USA | UK

Made with ❤ on the BookLeaf Publishing Platform
www.bookleafpub.in
www.bookleafpub.com

Dedication

To those who find beauty in the ordinary and solace in words.

Preface

These poems draw inspiration from nature, human experiences, relationships, and the world around us. They are snapshots of fleeting moments, capturing the essence of what it means to be alive in this ever-changing tapestry of existence. Poetry has the power to connect us across time and space, revealing shared truths and unique perspectives.

Acknowledgements

To my family and friends, thank you for your unwavering encouragement and belief in my words.

Unforgettable

I want to disappear so profoundly that not even the wind
will remember my name
The paths I have walked will not cry at my absence
The people I know cannot recall
Not even my face
And God will forgive
But he won't forget

Tears In A Bottle

Her heart is sticky like sun-flavored rum
Like peach-flavored candies I can't get off my tongue
Sour-sweet fables
And tails of the trees
A candle burning just for me
Her soft will of whisky
With peppermint drops
A lost little girl
Gin on the rocks
She sings for the trees
They dare her to run
Her protectors can't parent
As they do with weed
Nothing to give except needles from their sleeves
She was never thinking only dreaming
A heartbroken girl healed by twine
With cigarettes in the rain
And whisky now a bottle
Broken shards with beaten eyes
Cinnamon sticks and children cries
Candy wrappers and calloused hands
Bee stings and blood with wine
A paint palette of bruises

A heart broken by the hand of a man who was there to heal

Overused

I am a closed book with a cracked spine, ripped pages, faded words, and no story to tell

Green

I look with these eyes of green filling with envy
Just wishing I could be one of the many
Who doesn't have to keep telling themselves that they're
ok
I just wish one day
Looking in the mirror wouldn't hurt so bad like my
body's on display

Bonfire

Under the stars
Just with you
There's a bonfire
Dancing with the moon
Looking in your eyes
I know
My person is you

Casket of Memories

I fear
I've wasted my time
Watering flowers
That were already dead

Back to Fremont Road

When I die
Take me back
To my hometown
With the wild poppies
Booming
On the side of old Fremont road
As cigar smoke burns your nose
And breath seems to slow
The wild poppies dancing
In the wind
As I hold hands
With the sun

1000 Poems

I have a thousand poems in my head
Not even paper can comprehend
Words stuck waiting
Memories replaying
From the time
I wanted
To end it all

Wild Beauty

Little gap in her two front teeth
Running around on her concrete feet
She finds answers in the rain
And the sound of the sun
Just a little girl dancing for fun
Glances become stares
For her estranged wild beauty
Flowers seem to bloom
And hold their stalks high
As her fingernails are painted the same as the sky
Her only friend
Speaks through breeze
Soft forbidden melodies
Only she can seize
Wildflowers wrapped
In her little hands
Pollon on her nose
Only the wind knows
How far she'll go

Busted Lip

I can't form the words I want to say but I know you'll always be there when I'm not ok

You've helped me on the days I couldn't walk and found my voice when I refused to talk

Even with my busted lip you pulled me close and gave me a kiss

River

Morning doves cooing
Water rippling downstream
She wakes from the moon
In an old trailer she resides
She's one with the waves and dirty shorelines
She’s up with the dew
But she’s still not cold
The river is waiting
To grip her in its hold
She likes to swim and look at the moon
And that's exactly what she came to do

Amber Sunlight

Amber sunlight
Humming through trees
As the wind whispers
An old tune melody
Smokey leaves
Gathered up high
Almost so tall
They kiss the sky
Wildwood spring
In an old school town
Seasoned with past
But history not found

Colors

When I look
Into peoples eyes
I don’t know why
I feel like crying
It’s as though
I see
Not eyes
But
Different colors of regret

Feeling

I want to feel

But when I feel

I feel too much

Lost Soul

I am a lost soul
Wandering around
Hoping for the best
While knowing my best
Isn't enough

Wasted Years

I fear

I have wasted my years

Trying to be someone

That didn't exist

Fremont

There's a house on Fremont I go to see
It has a yellow body with a blue door and a thirsty-
looking tree
If you look from a certain way you can see the Oak
Glenn mounds cascading onto the background filling the
blank space with green
The backyard is full of wildflowers in spring and little
yellow weeds in late summers of July
You can feel the loose dirt sticking to your skin when
you pass by
A desolate road that reaches the sky
A little piece of the past waiting for its time

Broken Thumbs

You were like a breath of cigarette smoke
You made my eyes water and I started to choke
Voice laced with whisky
A hint of rum
You'll never stop playing the guitar on your broken
thumbs
Eyes of green, gold, and baby blue
The only person I've ever wanted was you

Keep The TV On

I like to listen to the tv while I sleep
It makes me feel less alone
Like there's someone there
I'm not alone
A pixled companion
I will never meet
They give me security in my time of sleep
The familiar hum
Of what it means
To be human
In a world of isolation

Grandpa Never Really Left

You visit me in my dreams
Yet it still feels I'm tearing at the seams
Like the old teddy bear you gave me now rich with tears
This has always been one of my biggest fears
You were here one day and gone the next
You still come and see me
Letting me know you're ok
You tell me there's a big place in heaven for you to stay
Your memories aren't gone
And your joints aren't weak
You don't get frustrated when you try to speak
Marvin Gaye is playing
And everyone is ok
Still singing and dancing
lighting up a room
With your bright smile you never got to lose

Judged

My biggest fear
Is for someone to judge me
In the way I judge myself

www.ingramcontent.com/pod-product-compliance
Lightning Source LLC
Chambersburg PA
CBHW052256170925
32785CB00029B/194
* 9 7 8 9 3 7 0 9 2 3 7 9 9 *